Contents

In the rockpool

Many creatures live in
rockpools along the seashore.
When the tide is out, there
may not be much water
inside the pool. When the
tide is in, the rockpool fills
up and bright anemones
uncurl their tentacles.

shell

rockpool at
low tide

starfish

4

1. A hermit crab lives inside the empty shell of a sea snail. The hard shell protects the crab's soft body.

2. The anemone sticks out its poisonous tentacles, which sting tiny sea creatures and push them towards its mouth.

3. Limpets, barnacles and mussels grow shells and attach themselves to rocks.

anemone's tentacles

Creatures that cling to rocks

limpets

barnacles

mussels

5

On the salt marsh

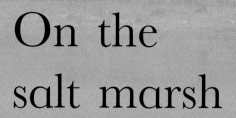

When the sea floods the land, salty marshes can form. Thick with rushes and reeds, they are home to many different birds, including flamingos.

flamingo chick

1. A flamingo stands on one leg to keep warm and dry, and to rest.

2. Flamingos are pink because they eat so many pink shrimps!

3. As well as birds, insects and snakes hide among the watery plants of salt marshes.

Other animals on the salt marsh

green-winged teal

dragonfly

Gulf water snake

7

Snowy seashores

In the coldest parts of the
world, animals live by the
sea to hunt for food in its icy
waters. Thick layers of fat,
fur or feathers keep the
animals warm.

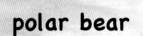

polar bear

male walrus
(a bull)

mother walrus
and her pup

1. A polar bear lives on the ice so that it can hunt seals for food.

2. Walruses have tusks and whiskers. A mother walrus has shorter tusks than a male walrus. A baby walrus has no tusks at all.

3. Some penguins slide down icy slopes on their bellies to splash into the sea.

Penguins like to...

waddle

slide on their stomachs

and dive into the water!

9

On the beach

When a wave washes up the beach, it drops shells and seaweed onto the sand. The wave also leaves behind tiny creatures for crabs and wading birds to eat.

hungry seagulls

sandcastle

crab

mermaid's purse

hidden starfish

10

1. Why are crabs tricky
   for seagulls to catch?

2. How many legs does
   a starfish have?

3. What can you find
   on the beach?

1. Crabs are tricky to catch because they have hard shells. They also move sideways, which confuses birds.

2. A starfish usually has five legs. If a crab or fish eats one leg, the starfish may grow another!

3. Pretty seashells and clumps of slimy seaweed wash up on the beach. If you see a jellyfish, don't touch it – it can sting!

shells

seaweed

jellyfish

Salty swamps

In hot parts of the world, salty swamps called mangroves meet the sea. Filled with plants and trees, they are home to fish, frogs, crabs and furry animals such as monkeys and otters.

fishing cat

long-tailed macaque monkeys

12

1. Do monkeys swim
in the sea?

2. How does a fishing cat
catch fish?

3. How do smooth-coated
otters look after
their babies?

jumping

splashing about

1. Some monkeys swim in the sea to cool down or to hunt fish and crabs for dinner.

2. The cat taps the water with its paw, pretending to be an insect. When a fish comes to investigate, the cat scoops it out.

3. The mother and father otters dig a burrow near water. The babies are born inside the burrow.

Looking after baby otters

mother and father otters

otter pups outside burrow

learning to swim

13

Rocky islands

Many seashore animals live on islands far out at sea. They have their babies on land, among the rocks and cliffs, but dive deep into the ocean to find food.

iguanas sunbathing

14

1. Which lizards live
by the sea?

2. Why are some marine
iguanas pink and white?

3. Where do puffins make
their nests?

spraying
salt

1. Marine iguanas dive into the cold sea to eat sea plants. They sunbathe on rocks to warm up again.

2. Some male marine iguanas turn pink to attract females. All the lizards spray sea salt out of their noses. This makes their faces white!

3. Puffins dig nests by digging burrows on a grassy cliff top.

How puffins live on cliffs

mother and baby chick

inside a burrow

diving for fish

15

Night-time on the beach

The seashore can be safer for some animals at night. Predators (animals that hunt other animals) find it hard to hunt in the darkness. Bats, however, are excellent night-time hunters.

loggerhead turtle

1. Why does a turtle
like the beach?

2. How many eggs does
a loggerhead turtle lay?

3. Which 'fisherman'
hunts at night?

1. A turtle likes to lay her eggs in a sandy burrow on a beach.

2. The turtle lays about 100 eggs. They look like ping-pong balls!

laying eggs

3. A fisherman bat hunts at night. It flies along the beach and snatches up fish with its feet.

How a fisherman bat hunts

swooping across water

snatching up a fish

flying away

17

Index

A
anemones 4, 5

B
barnacles 5
bats 16, 17
beaches 10–11, 16–17

C
crabs 5, 10, 11

F
flamingos 6, 7

H
hunting 8, 9, 13, 16

I
ice 8–9
iguanas 14, 15
islands 14

J
jellyfish 11

L
limpets 5

M
monkeys 12, 13
mussels 5

N
night 16–17

O
otters 13

P
penguins 9
puffins 15

R
rockpools 4–5

S
salt marshes 6–7
shells 5, 10, 11
starfish 4, 11
swamps 12–13

T
tides 4
turtles 16, 17

W
walruses 8, 9
waves 10